MznLnx

Missing Links Exam Preps

Exam Prep for

Escaping the Black Hole: Minimizing the Damage from the Marketing-Sales Disconnect

Schmonsees, 1st Edition

The MznLnx Exam Prep is your link from the texbook and lecture to your exams.
The MznLnx Exam Preps are unauthorized and comprehensive reviews of your textbooks.

All material provided by MznLnx and Rico Publications (c) 2010
Textbook publishers and textbook authors do not particpate in or contribute to these reviews.

MznLnx

Rico
Publications

Exam Prep for Escaping the Black Hole: Minimizing the Damage from the Marketing-Sales Disconnect
1st Edition
Schmonsees

Publisher: Raymond Houge
Assistant Editor: Michael Rouger
Text and Cover Designer: Lisa Buckner
Marketing Manager: Sara Swagger
Project Manager, Editorial Production: Jerry Emerson
Art Director: Vernon Lowerui

Product Manager: Dave Mason
Editorial Assitant: Rachel Guzmanji
Pedagogy: Debra Long
Cover Image: Jim Reed/Getty Images
Text and Cover Printer: City Printing, Inc.
Compositor: Media Mix, Inc.

(c) 2010 Rico Publications

ALL RIGHTS RESERVED. No part of this work covered by the copyright may be reproduced or used in any form or by an means--graphic, electronic, or mechanical, including photocopying, recording, taping, Web distribution, information storage, and retrieval systems, or in any other manner--without the written permission of the publisher.

Printed in the United States
ISBN:

For more information about our products, contact us at:
Dave.Mason@RicoPublications.com

For permission to use material from this text or product, submit a request online to:
Dave.Mason@RicoPublications.com

Contents

CHAPTER 1
The Schwarzschild Radius — 1

CHAPTER 2
The Increasing Market Complexity — 3

CHAPTER 3
The Changing Market Dynamics — 4

CHAPTER 4
The Changing Communications Model — 6

CHAPTER 5
Understanding the Disconnect — 9

CHAPTER 6
Strategic Mistakes — 13

CHAPTER 7
Missed Opportunities — 16

CHAPTER 8
Alignment as a Core Strategy — 19

CHAPTER 9
Conceptualizing the Ecosystem — 22

CHAPTER 10
Discovering the Holy Grail — 24

CHAPTER 11
Enabling the Ecosystem — 26

CHAPTER 12
Understanding the Model — 27

CHAPTER 13
Integrated Pipeline Management — 28

CHAPTER 14
Understanding the Model — 30

CHAPTER 15
Adopting the VCCM — 32

CHAPTER 16
Building a Value Map — 34

CHAPTER 17
Optimizing the Sanctioned Content — 35

ANSWER KEY — 40

TO THE STUDENT

COMPREHENSIVE

The *MznLnx* Exam Prep series is designed to help you pass your exams. Editors at MznLnx review your textbooks and then prepare these practice exams to help you master the textbook material. Unlike study guides, workbooks, and practice tests provided by the texbook publisher and textbook authors, *MznLnx* gives you **all** of the material in each chapter in exam form, not just samples, so you can be sure to nail your exam.

MECHANICAL

The MznLnx Exam Prep series creates exams that will help you learn the subject matter as well as test you on your understanding. Each question is designed to help you master the concept. Just working through the exams, you gain an understanding of the subject--its a simple mechanical process that produces success.

INTEGRATED STUDY GUIDE AND REVIEW

MznLnx is not just a set of exams designed to test you, its also a comprehensive review of the subject content. Each exam question is also a review of the concept, making sure that you will get the answer correct without having to go to other sources of material. You learn as you go! Its the easiest way to pass an exam.

HUMOR

Studying can be tedious and dry. MznLnx's instructional design includes moderate humor within the exam questions on occassion, to break the tedium and revitalize the brain

Chapter 1. The Schwarzschild Radius

1. _____ is defined by the American _____ Association as the activity, set of institutions, and processes for creating, communicating, delivering, and exchanging offerings that have value for customers, clients, partners, and society at large. The term developed from the original meaning which referred literally to going to market, as in shopping, or going to a market to sell goods or services.

_____ practice tends to be seen as a creative industry, which includes advertising, distribution and selling.

a. Marketing myopia
b. Marketing
c. Product naming
d. Customer acquisition management

2. _____, in marketing and sales, is the collection of media used to support the sales of a product or service. These sales aids are intended to make the sales effort easier and more effective. The brand of the company usually presents itself by way of its collateral to enhance its brand.
a. 180SearchAssistant
b. Product churning
c. Power III
d. Marketing collateral

3. Importance of _____ is critical for any commercial organization. Expanding business is not possible without increasing sales volumes, and effective _____ goal is to organize sales team work in such a manner that ensures a growing flow of regular customers and increasing amount of sales.

The four phase-model of Management Process

1. Conception
2. Planning
3. Execution
4. Control

This model is cyclical, so it is a constant/continuous process.

===_____ is attainment of sales force goals in a effective ' efficient manner through planning, staffing, training, leading ' controlling organizational resources.

a. Sales management
b. Sales process
c. Request for proposal
d. Hit rate

Chapter 1. The Schwarzschild Radius

4. In calculus, a function f defined on a subset of the real numbers with real values is called _____, if for all x and y such that x ≤ y one has f(x) ≤ f(y), so f preserves the order. In layman's terms, the sign of the slope is always positive (the curve tending upwards) or zero (i.e., non-decreasing, or asymptotic, or depicted as a horizontal, flat line) Likewise, a function is called monotonically decreasing (non-increasing) if, whenever x ≤ y, then f(x) ≥ f(y), so it reverses the order.
   a. 6-3-5 Brainwriting
   b. 180SearchAssistant
   c. Power III
   d. Monotonic

5. The _____ is a professional association for marketers. As of 2008 it had approximately 40,000 members. There are collegiate chapters on 250 campuses.
   a. American Marketing Association
   b. ACNielsen
   c. AMAX
   d. ADTECH

Chapter 2. The Increasing Market Complexity

1. _____ is defined by the American _____ Association as the activity, set of institutions, and processes for creating, communicating, delivering, and exchanging offerings that have value for customers, clients, partners, and society at large. The term developed from the original meaning which referred literally to going to market, as in shopping, or going to a market to sell goods or services.

_____ practice tends to be seen as a creative industry, which includes advertising, distribution and selling.

   a. Marketing myopia
   b. Marketing
   c. Customer acquisition management
   d. Product naming

2. _____, in marketing and sales, is the collection of media used to support the sales of a product or service. These sales aids are intended to make the sales effort easier and more effective. The brand of the company usually presents itself by way of its collateral to enhance its brand.
   a. Product churning
   b. Power III
   c. 180SearchAssistant
   d. Marketing collateral

3. _____ is one of the four elements of marketing mix. An organization or set of organizations (go-betweens) involved in the process of making a product or service available for use or consumption by a consumer or business user.

The other three parts of the marketing mix are product, pricing, and promotion.

   a. Distribution
   b. Better Living Through Chemistry
   c. Japan Advertising Photographers' Association
   d. Comparison-Shopping agent

Chapter 3. The Changing Market Dynamics

1. _____ is an advertisement in which a particular product specifically mentions a competitor by name for the express purpose of showing why the competitor is inferior to the product naming it.

This should not be confused with parody advertisements, where a fictional product is being advertised for the purpose of poking fun at the particular advertisement, nor should it be confused with the use of a coined brand name for the purpose of comparing the product without actually naming an actual competitor. ('Wikipedia tastes better and is less filling than the Encyclopedia Galactica.')

In the 1980s, during what has been referred to as the cola wars, soft-drink manufacturer Pepsi ran a series of advertisements where people, caught on hidden camera, in a blind taste test, chose Pepsi over rival Coca-Cola.

   a. Comparative advertising
   b. Cost per conversion
   c. GL-70
   d. Heavy-up

2. _____ is that length of time that food, drink, medicine and other perishable items are given before they are considered unsuitable for sale or consumption. In some regions, a best before, use by or freshness date is required on packaged perishable foods.

_____ is the recommendation of time that products can be stored, during which the defined quality of a specified proportion of the goods remains acceptable under expected (or specified) conditions of distribution, storage and display.

   a. 180SearchAssistant
   b. Power III
   c. Food safety
   d. Shelf life

3. A personal and cultural _____ is a relative ethic _____, an assumption upon which implementation can be extrapolated. A _____ system is a set of consistent _____s and measures that is soo not true. A principle _____ is a foundation upon which other _____s and measures of integrity are based.
   a. Value
   b. Perceptual maps
   c. Supreme Court of the United States
   d. Package-on-Package

4. In the field of marketing, a customer _____ consists of the sum total of benefits which a vendor promises that a customer will receive in return for the customer's associated payment (or other value-transfer.)

Put simply, the _____ is what the customer gets for his money.

Accordingly, a customer can evaluate a company's value-proposition on two broad dimensions with multiple subsets:

1. relative performance: what the customer gets from the vendor relative to a competitor's offering;
2. price: which consists of the payment the customer makes to acquire the product or service; plus the access cost

The vendor-company's marketing and sales efforts offer a customer _____; the vendor-company's delivery and customer-service processes then fulfill that value-proposition.

A value-proposition can assist in a firm's marketing strategy, and may guide a business to target a particular market segment.

a. Marketing performance measurement and management
b. DefCom Australia
c. Relationship management
d. Value Proposition

Chapter 4. The Changing Communications Model

1. Advertising mail junk mail is the delivery of advertising material to recipients of postal mail. The delivery of advertising mail forms a large and growing service for many postal services, and _____ marketing forms a significant portion of the direct marketing industry. Some organizations attempt to help people opt-out of receiving advertising mail, in many cases motivated by a concern over its negative environmental impact.
   a. Phishing
   b. Telemarketing
   c. Directory Harvest Attack
   d. Direct mail

2. _____ is defined by the American _____ Association as the activity, set of institutions, and processes for creating, communicating, delivering, and exchanging offerings that have value for customers, clients, partners, and society at large. The term developed from the original meaning which referred literally to going to market, as in shopping, or going to a market to sell goods or services.

   _____ practice tends to be seen as a creative industry, which includes advertising, distribution and selling.

   a. Marketing myopia
   b. Product naming
   c. Customer acquisition management
   d. Marketing

3. In economics, business, retail, and accounting, a _____ is the value of money that has been used up to produce something, and hence is not available for use anymore. In economics, a _____ is an alternative that is given up as a result of a decision. In business, the _____ may be one of acquisition, in which case the amount of money expended to acquire it is counted as _____.
   a. Fixed costs
   b. Transaction cost
   c. Variable cost
   d. Cost

4. _____, sometimes referred to as information richness theory, is a framework that can be used to describe a communications medium by describing its ability to reproduce the information sent over it. It was developed by Richard L. Daft and Robert H. Lengel. For example, a phone call will not be able to reproduce visual social cues such as gestures.
   a. 6-3-5 Brainwriting
   b. Power III
   c. 180SearchAssistant
   d. Media richness theory

Chapter 4. The Changing Communications Model

5. A personal and cultural _____ is a relative ethic _____, an assumption upon which implementation can be extrapolated. A _____ system is a set of consistent _____s and measures that is soo not true. A principle _____ is a foundation upon which other _____s and measures of integrity are based.
   a. Supreme Court of the United States
   b. Perceptual maps
   c. Package-on-Package
   d. Value

6. In the field of marketing, a customer _____ consists of the sum total of benefits which a vendor promises that a customer will receive in return for the customer's associated payment (or other value-transfer.)

Put simply, the _____ is what the customer gets for his money.

Accordingly, a customer can evaluate a company's value-proposition on two broad dimensions with multiple subsets:

   1. relative performance: what the customer gets from the vendor relative to a competitor's offering;
   2. price: which consists of the payment the customer makes to acquire the product or service; plus the access cost

The vendor-company's marketing and sales efforts offer a customer _____; the vendor-company's delivery and customer-service processes then fulfill that value-proposition.

A value-proposition can assist in a firm's marketing strategy, and may guide a business to target a particular market segment.

   a. Marketing performance measurement and management
   b. DefCom Australia
   c. Relationship management
   d. Value Proposition

7. A _____ is a type of website, usually maintained by an individual with regular entries of commentary, descriptions of events, or other material such as graphics or video. Entries are commonly displayed in reverse-chronological order. '_____' can also be used as a verb, meaning to maintain or add content to a _____.
   a. 6-3-5 Brainwriting
   b. Power III
   c. 180SearchAssistant
   d. Blog

Chapter 4. The Changing Communications Model

8. _____ is a recursive process where two or more people or organizations work together toward an intersection of common goals -- for example, an intellectual endeavor that is creative in nature--by sharing knowledge, learning and building consensus. _____ does not require leadership and can sometimes bring better results through decentralization and egalitarianism. In particular, teams that work collaboratively can obtain greater resources, recognition and reward when facing competition for finite resources._____ is also present in opposing goals exhibiting the notion of adversarial _____, though this notion is atypical of the annotation that people have given towards their understanding of _____.
   a. Power III
   b. 180SearchAssistant
   c. 6-3-5 Brainwriting
   d. Collaboration

9. The _____ is a professional association for marketers. As of 2008 it had approximately 40,000 members. There are collegiate chapters on 250 campuses.
   a. ACNielsen
   b. ADTECH
   c. American Marketing Association
   d. AMAX

Chapter 5. Understanding the Disconnect

1. _____ is defined by the American _____ Association as the activity, set of institutions, and processes for creating, communicating, delivering, and exchanging offerings that have value for customers, clients, partners, and society at large. The term developed from the original meaning which referred literally to going to market, as in shopping, or going to a market to sell goods or services.

   _____ practice tends to be seen as a creative industry, which includes advertising, distribution and selling.

   a. Customer acquisition management
   b. Marketing myopia
   c. Product naming
   d. Marketing

2. _____s or previews are film advertisements for feature films that will be exhibited in the future at a cinema, on whose screen they are shown. The term '_____' comes from their having originally been shown at the end of a film programme. That practice did not last long, because patrons tended to leave the theater after the films ended, but the name has stuck.
   a. Distribution
   b. Trailer
   c. Rural market
   d. Clustering

3. A personal and cultural _____ is a relative ethic _____, an assumption upon which implementation can be extrapolated. A _____ system is a set of consistent _____s and measures that is soo not true. A principle _____ is a foundation upon which other _____s and measures of integrity are based.
   a. Supreme Court of the United States
   b. Perceptual maps
   c. Package-on-Package
   d. Value

4. In the field of marketing, a customer _____ consists of the sum total of benefits which a vendor promises that a customer will receive in return for the customer's associated payment (or other value-transfer.)

   Put simply, the _____ is what the customer gets for his money.

   Accordingly, a customer can evaluate a company's value-proposition on two broad dimensions with multiple subsets:

   1. relative performance: what the customer gets from the vendor relative to a competitor's offering;
   2. price: which consists of the payment the customer makes to acquire the product or service; plus the access cost

Chapter 5. Understanding the Disconnect

The vendor-company's marketing and sales efforts offer a customer _____; the vendor-company's delivery and customer-service processes then fulfill that value-proposition.

A value-proposition can assist in a firm's marketing strategy, and may guide a business to target a particular market segment.

   a. Marketing performance measurement and management
   b. Value proposition
   c. Relationship management
   d. DefCom Australia

5. In calculus, a function f defined on a subset of the real numbers with real values is called _____, if for all x and y such that x ≤ y one has f(x) ≤ f(y), so f preserves the order. In layman's terms, the sign of the slope is always positive (the curve tending upwards) or zero (i.e., non-decreasing, or asymptotic, or depicted as a horizontal, flat line) Likewise, a function is called monotonically decreasing (non-increasing) if, whenever x ≤ y, then f(x) ≥ f(y), so it reverses the order.
   a. 180SearchAssistant
   b. 6-3-5 Brainwriting
   c. Power III
   d. Monotonic

6. In economics, _____ is the desire to own something and the ability to pay for it. The term _____ signifies the ability or the willingness to buy a particular commodity at a given point of time .

   a. Market system
   b. Demand
   c. Market dominance
   d. Discretionary spending

7. _____ is the focus of targeted marketing programs to drive awareness and interest in a company's products and/or services. Commonly used in business to business, business to government, or longer sales cycle business to consumer sales cycles, _____ involves multiple areas of marketing and is really the marriage of marketing programs coupled with a structured sales process.

There are multiple components of a stepped _____ process that vary based on the size and complexity of a sale.

Chapter 5. Understanding the Disconnect

a. Demand generation
b. Marketing performance measurement and management
c. Bitcom
d. Blind taste test

8. In marketing, _____ has come to mean the process by which marketers try to create an image or identity in the minds of their target market for its product, brand, or organization. It is the 'relative competitive comparison' their product occupies in a given market as perceived by the target market.

Re-_____ involves changing the identity of a product, relative to the identity of competing products, in the collective minds of the target market.

a. Moratorium
b. Containerization
c. Positioning
d. GE matrix

9. _____ is the state or fact of exclusive rights and control over property, which may be an object, land/real estate, or some other kind of property (like government-granted monopolies collectively referred to as intellectual property.) It is embodied in an _____ right also referred to as title.

_____ is the key building block in the development of the capitalist socio-economic system.

a. Ownership
b. ADTECH
c. AMAX
d. ACNielsen

10. Human beings are also considered to be _____ because they have the ability to change raw materials into valuable _____. The term Human _____ can also be defined as the skills, energies, talents, abilities and knowledge that are used for the production of goods or the rendering of services. While taking into account human beings as _____, the following things have to be kept in mind:

- The size of the population
- The capabilities of the individuals in that population

Many _____ cannot be consumed in their original form. They have to be processed in order to change them into more usable commodities.

a. 180SearchAssistant
b. 6-3-5 Brainwriting
c. Power III
d. Resources

Chapter 6. Strategic Mistakes

1. _____ is a technique used in propaganda and advertising. Also known as association, this is a technique of projecting positive or negative qualities (praise or blame) of a person, entity, object, or value (an individual, group, organization, nation, patriotism, etc.) to another in order to make the second more acceptable or to discredit it.
   a. Supplier
   b. Transfer
   c. Sexism,
   d. Micro ads

2. A personal and cultural _____ is a relative ethic _____, an assumption upon which implementation can be extrapolated. A _____ system is a set of consistent _____s and measures that is soo not true. A principle _____ is a foundation upon which other _____s and measures of integrity are based.
   a. Package-on-Package
   b. Perceptual maps
   c. Supreme Court of the United States
   d. Value

3. In the field of marketing, a customer _____ consists of the sum total of benefits which a vendor promises that a customer will receive in return for the customer's associated payment (or other value-transfer.)

Put simply, the _____ is what the customer gets for his money.

Accordingly, a customer can evaluate a company's value-proposition on two broad dimensions with multiple subsets:

   1. relative performance: what the customer gets from the vendor relative to a competitor's offering;
   2. price: which consists of the payment the customer makes to acquire the product or service; plus the access cost

The vendor-company's marketing and sales efforts offer a customer _____; the vendor-company's delivery and customer-service processes then fulfill that value-proposition.

A value-proposition can assist in a firm's marketing strategy, and may guide a business to target a particular market segment.

   a. Relationship management
   b. Value proposition
   c. Marketing performance measurement and management
   d. DefCom Australia

Chapter 6. Strategic Mistakes

4. _____ is a business management strategy, originally developed by Motorola, that today enjoys widespread application in many sectors of industry.

_____ seeks to identify and remove the causes of defects and errors in manufacturing and business processes. It uses a set of quality management methods, including statistical methods, and creates a special infrastructure of people within the organization ('Black Belts' etc.)

   a. Six Sigma
   b. Power III
   c. 6-3-5 Brainwriting
   d. 180SearchAssistant

5. _____ is a business management strategy aimed at embedding awareness of quality in all organizational processes. _____ has been widely used in manufacturing, education, call centers, government, and service industries, as well as NASA space and science programs.

When used together as a phrase, the three words in this expression have the following meanings:

- Total: Involving the entire organization, supply chain, and/or product life cycle
- Quality: With its usual definitions, with all its complexities
- Management: The system of managing with steps like Plan, Organize, Control, Lead, Staff, provisioning and organizing.

As defined by the International Organization for Standardization (ISO):

'_____ is a management approach for an organization, centered on quality, based on the participation of all its members and aiming at long-term success through customer satisfaction, and benefits to all members of the organization and to society.' ISO 8402:1994

One major aim is to reduce variation from every process so that greater consistency of effort is obtained. (Royse, D., Thyer, B., Padgett D., ' Logan T., 2006)

In Japan, _____ comprises four process steps, namely:

1. Kaizen - Focuses on 'Continuous Process Improvement', to make processes visible, repeatable and measurable.
2. Atarimae Hinshitsu - The idea that 'things will work as they are supposed to' .
3. Kansei - Examining the way the user applies the product leads to improvement in the product itself.
4. Miryokuteki Hinshitsu - The idea that 'things should have an aesthetic quality' (for example, a pen will write in a way that is pleasing to the writer.)

_____ requires that the company maintain this quality standard in all aspects of its business. This requires ensuring that things are done right the first time and that defects and waste are eliminated from operations.

a. 180SearchAssistant
b. 6-3-5 Brainwriting
c. Power III
d. Total Quality Management

Chapter 7. Missed Opportunities

1. A personal and cultural _____ is a relative ethic _____, an assumption upon which implementation can be extrapolated. A _____ system is a set of consistent _____s and measures that is soo not true. A principle _____ is a foundation upon which other _____s and measures of integrity are based.
   a. Supreme Court of the United States
   b. Package-on-Package
   c. Perceptual maps
   d. Value

2. _____ is a worldwide management consulting firm that focuses on solving issues of concern to senior management. McKinsey serves as an advisor to the world's leading businesses, governments, and institutions. It is widely recognized as a leader and one of the most prestigious firms in the management consulting industry.
   a. 180SearchAssistant
   b. Power III
   c. 6-3-5 Brainwriting
   d. McKinsey ' Company

3. _____ is defined by the American _____ Association as the activity, set of institutions, and processes for creating, communicating, delivering, and exchanging offerings that have value for customers, clients, partners, and society at large. The term developed from the original meaning which referred literally to going to market, as in shopping, or going to a market to sell goods or services.

   _____ practice tends to be seen as a creative industry, which includes advertising, distribution and selling.

   a. Marketing myopia
   b. Customer acquisition management
   c. Product naming
   d. Marketing

4. A _____ researches, selects, develops, and places a company's products.

   A _____ considers numerous factors such as target demographic, the products offered by the competition, and how well the product fits in with the company's business model. Generally, a _____ manages one or more tangible products.

   a. Power III
   b. Promotional mix
   c. Pick and pack
   d. Product Manager

Chapter 7. Missed Opportunities

5. In economics, business, retail, and accounting, a _____ is the value of money that has been used up to produce something, and hence is not available for use anymore. In economics, a _____ is an alternative that is given up as a result of a decision. In business, the _____ may be one of acquisition, in which case the amount of money expended to acquire it is counted as _____.
   a. Cost
   b. Fixed costs
   c. Variable cost
   d. Transaction cost

6. In economics, and cost accounting, _____ describes the total economic cost of production and is made up of variable costs, which vary according to the quantity of a good produced and include inputs such as labor and raw materials, plus fixed costs, which are independent of the quantity of a good produced and include inputs (capital) that cannot be varied in the short term, such as buildings and machinery. _____ in economics includes the total opportunity cost of each factor of production in addition to fixed and variable costs.

The rate at which _____ changes as the amount produced changes is called marginal cost.

   a. Total Cost
   b. Household production function
   c. Hoarding
   d. Product proliferation

7. In the field of marketing, a customer _____ consists of the sum total of benefits which a vendor promises that a customer will receive in return for the customer's associated payment (or other value-transfer.)

Put simply, the _____ is what the customer gets for his money.

Accordingly, a customer can evaluate a company's value-proposition on two broad dimensions with multiple subsets:

   1. relative performance: what the customer gets from the vendor relative to a competitor's offering;
   2. price: which consists of the payment the customer makes to acquire the product or service; plus the access cost

The vendor-company's marketing and sales efforts offer a customer _____; the vendor-company's delivery and customer-service processes then fulfill that value-proposition.

A value-proposition can assist in a firm's marketing strategy, and may guide a business to target a particular market segment.

a. Marketing performance measurement and management
b. Value Proposition
c. Relationship management
d. DefCom Australia

8. The _____ is a professional association for marketers. As of 2008 it had approximately 40,000 members. There are collegiate chapters on 250 campuses.
a. AMAX
b. ACNielsen
c. ADTECH
d. American Marketing Association

Chapter 8. Alignment as a Core Strategy

1. _____ is defined by the American _____ Association as the activity, set of institutions, and processes for creating, communicating, delivering, and exchanging offerings that have value for customers, clients, partners, and society at large. The term developed from the original meaning which referred literally to going to market, as in shopping, or going to a market to sell goods or services.

   _____ practice tends to be seen as a creative industry, which includes advertising, distribution and selling.

   a. Product naming
   b. Customer acquisition management
   c. Marketing myopia
   d. Marketing

2. A _____ is a plan of action designed to achieve a particular goal.

   _____ is different from tactics. In military terms, tactics is concerned with the conduct of an engagement while _____ is concerned with how different engagements are linked.

   a. Power III
   b. 6-3-5 Brainwriting
   c. Strategy
   d. 180SearchAssistant

3. _____ is a business management strategy, originally developed by Motorola, that today enjoys widespread application in many sectors of industry.

   _____ seeks to identify and remove the causes of defects and errors in manufacturing and business processes. It uses a set of quality management methods, including statistical methods, and creates a special infrastructure of people within the organization ('Black Belts' etc.)

   a. 180SearchAssistant
   b. 6-3-5 Brainwriting
   c. Six Sigma
   d. Power III

4. Importance of _____ is critical for any commercial organization. Expanding business is not possible without increasing sales volumes, and effective _____ goal is to organize sales team work in such a manner that ensures a growing flow of regular customers and increasing amount of sales.

Chapter 8. Alignment as a Core Strategy

The four phase-model of Management Process

1. Conception
2. Planning
3. Execution
4. Control

This model is cyclical, so it is a constant/continuous process.

===_____ is attainment of sales force goals in a effective ' efficient manner through planning, staffing, training, leading ' controlling organizational resources.

a. Sales management
b. Hit rate
c. Sales process
d. Request for proposal

5. _____ is a worldwide management consulting firm that focuses on solving issues of concern to senior management. McKinsey serves as an advisor to the world's leading businesses, governments, and institutions. It is widely recognized as a leader and one of the most prestigious firms in the management consulting industry.
    a. 6-3-5 Brainwriting
    b. McKinsey ' Company
    c. Power III
    d. 180SearchAssistant

6. The _____ is a professional association for marketers. As of 2008 it had approximately 40,000 members. There are collegiate chapters on 250 campuses.
    a. ADTECH
    b. AMAX
    c. ACNielsen
    d. American Marketing Association

7. In calculus, a function f defined on a subset of the real numbers with real values is called _____, if for all x and y such that $x \leq y$ one has $f(x) \leq f(y)$, so f preserves the order. In layman's terms, the sign of the slope is always positive (the curve tending upwards) or zero (i.e., non-decreasing, or asymptotic, or depicted as a horizontal, flat line) Likewise, a function is called monotonically decreasing (non-increasing) if, whenever $x \leq y$, then $f(x) \geq f(y)$, so it reverses the order.

a. Power III
b. 180SearchAssistant
c. 6-3-5 Brainwriting
d. Monotonic

8. _____ is a corporate title referring to an executive responsible for various marketing in an organization. Most often the position reports to the chief executive officer.

With primary or shared responsibility for areas such as sales management, product development, distribution channel management, public relations, marketing communications (including advertising and promotions), pricing, market research, and customer service.

a. Tudou
b. Chief Marketing Officer
c. Direct investment
d. MySpace

Chapter 9. Conceptualizing the Ecosystem

1. _____ is defined by the American _____ Association as the activity, set of institutions, and processes for creating, communicating, delivering, and exchanging offerings that have value for customers, clients, partners, and society at large. The term developed from the original meaning which referred literally to going to market, as in shopping, or going to a market to sell goods or services.

_____ practice tends to be seen as a creative industry, which includes advertising, distribution and selling.

   a. Product naming
   b. Marketing
   c. Customer acquisition management
   d. Marketing myopia

2. A personal and cultural _____ is a relative ethic _____, an assumption upon which implementation can be extrapolated. A _____ system is a set of consistent _____s and measures that is soo not true. A principle _____ is a foundation upon which other _____s and measures of integrity are based.
   a. Supreme Court of the United States
   b. Package-on-Package
   c. Perceptual maps
   d. Value

3. In the field of marketing, a customer _____ consists of the sum total of benefits which a vendor promises that a customer will receive in return for the customer's associated payment (or other value-transfer.)

Put simply, the _____ is what the customer gets for his money.

Accordingly, a customer can evaluate a company's value-proposition on two broad dimensions with multiple subsets:

   1. relative performance: what the customer gets from the vendor relative to a competitor's offering;
   2. price: which consists of the payment the customer makes to acquire the product or service; plus the access cost

The vendor-company's marketing and sales efforts offer a customer _____; the vendor-company's delivery and customer-service processes then fulfill that value-proposition.

A value-proposition can assist in a firm's marketing strategy, and may guide a business to target a particular market segment.

a. Relationship management
b. Marketing performance measurement and management
c. Value Proposition
d. DefCom Australia

4. The _____ is a performance management tool which began as a concept for measuring whether the smaller-scale operational activities of a company are aligned with its larger-scale objectives in terms of vision and strategy.

By focusing not only on financial outcomes but also on the operational, marketing and developmental inputs to these, the _____ helps provide a more comprehensive view of a business, which in turn helps organizations act in their best long-term interests.

Organizations were encouraged to measure, in addition to financial outputs, those factors which influenced the financial outputs.

a. Time management
b. Balanced Scorecard
c. Voice of the customer
d. Goal setting

5. _____ is a business management strategy, originally developed by Motorola, that today enjoys widespread application in many sectors of industry.

_____ seeks to identify and remove the causes of defects and errors in manufacturing and business processes. It uses a set of quality management methods, including statistical methods, and creates a special infrastructure of people within the organization ('Black Belts' etc.)

a. 6-3-5 Brainwriting
b. Power III
c. 180SearchAssistant
d. Six Sigma

Chapter 10. Discovering the Holy Grail

1. In marketing, _____ has come to mean the process by which marketers try to create an image or identity in the minds of their target market for its product, brand, or organization. It is the 'relative competitive comparison' their product occupies in a given market as perceived by the target market.

    Re-_____ involves changing the identity of a product, relative to the identity of competing products, in the collective minds of the target market.

    a. Moratorium
    b. GE matrix
    c. Containerization
    d. Positioning

2. A personal and cultural _____ is a relative ethic _____, an assumption upon which implementation can be extrapolated. A _____ system is a set of consistent _____s and measures that is soo not true. A principle _____ is a foundation upon which other _____s and measures of integrity are based.
    a. Value
    b. Supreme Court of the United States
    c. Perceptual maps
    d. Package-on-Package

3. In the field of marketing, a customer _____ consists of the sum total of benefits which a vendor promises that a customer will receive in return for the customer's associated payment (or other value-transfer.)

    Put simply, the _____ is what the customer gets for his money.

    Accordingly, a customer can evaluate a company's value-proposition on two broad dimensions with multiple subsets:

    1. relative performance: what the customer gets from the vendor relative to a competitor's offering;
    2. price: which consists of the payment the customer makes to acquire the product or service; plus the access cost

    The vendor-company's marketing and sales efforts offer a customer _____; the vendor-company's delivery and customer-service processes then fulfill that value-proposition.

    A value-proposition can assist in a firm's marketing strategy, and may guide a business to target a particular market segment.

a. Marketing performance measurement and management
b. DefCom Australia
c. Relationship management
d. Value Proposition

4. _____ is the realization of an application idea, model, design, specification, standard, algorithm an _____ is a realization of a technical specification or algorithm as a program, software component, or other computer system. Many _____s may exist for a given specification or standard.
   a. ADTECH
   b. ACNielsen
   c. AMAX
   d. Implementation

1. _____ is the realization of an application idea, model, design, specification, standard, algorithm an _____ is a realization of a technical specification or algorithm as a program, software component, or other computer system. Many _____s may exist for a given specification or standard.
    a. Implementation
    b. ACNielsen
    c. AMAX
    d. ADTECH

Chapter 12. Understanding the Model

1. In economics, _____ is the desire to own something and the ability to pay for it. The term _____ signifies the ability or the willingness to buy a particular commodity at a given point of time .

   a. Discretionary spending
   b. Demand
   c. Market dominance
   d. Market system

2. _____ is the focus of targeted marketing programs to drive awareness and interest in a company's products and/or services. Commonly used in business to business, business to government, or longer sales cycle business to consumer sales cycles, _____ involves multiple areas of marketing and is really the marriage of marketing programs coupled with a structured sales process.

   There are multiple components of a stepped _____ process that vary based on the size and complexity of a sale.

   a. Demand generation
   b. Marketing performance measurement and management
   c. Blind taste test
   d. Bitcom

3. A personal and cultural _____ is a relative ethic _____, an assumption upon which implementation can be extrapolated. A _____ system is a set of consistent _____s and measures that is soo not true. A principle _____ is a foundation upon which other _____s and measures of integrity are based.
   a. Perceptual maps
   b. Supreme Court of the United States
   c. Package-on-Package
   d. Value

Chapter 13. Integrated Pipeline Management

1. _____ describes the situation when output from (or information about the result of) an event or phenomenon in the past will influence the same event/phenomenon in the present or future. When an event is part of a chain of cause-and-effect that forms a circuit or loop, then the event is said to 'feed back' into itself.

   _____ is also a synonym for:

   - _____ Signal; the information about the initial event that is the basis for subsequent modification of the event.
   - _____ Loop; the causal path that leads from the initial generation of the _____ signal to the subsequent modification of the event.

   _____ is a mechanism, process or signal that is looped back to control a system within itself. Such a loop is called a _____ loop.

   a. Power III
   b. Feedback
   c. 180SearchAssistant
   d. 6-3-5 Brainwriting

2. _____ defines a category of software used by marketing organizations to manage their end-to-end process from gathering and analyzing customer data across websites and other channels, to planning, budgeting and managing the creative production process, to executing targeted customer communications to measuring results and effectiveness. _____ is a superset of other marketing software categories such as Web Analytics, Campaign Management, Marketing Resource Management, Marketing Dashboards, Lead Management, Event-driven Marketing, Predictive Modeling and more. The goal of deploying and using _____ is to improve both the efficiency and effectiveness of marketing by increasing revenue generation, decreasing costs and waste, and reducing time to market.
   a. Electronic retailing self-regulation program
   b. Advertising media selection
   c. ACNielsen
   d. Enterprise Marketing Management

3. In economics, an externality or spillover of an economic transaction is an impact on a party that is not directly involved in the transaction. In such a case, prices do not reflect the full costs or benefits in production or consumption of a product or service. A positive impact is called an _____ benefit, while a negative impact is called an _____ cost.
   a. ADTECH
   b. ACNielsen
   c. AMAX
   d. External

Chapter 13. Integrated Pipeline Management

4. _____ is defined by the American _____ Association as the activity, set of institutions, and processes for creating, communicating, delivering, and exchanging offerings that have value for customers, clients, partners, and society at large. The term developed from the original meaning which referred literally to going to market, as in shopping, or going to a market to sell goods or services.

_____ practice tends to be seen as a creative industry, which includes advertising, distribution and selling.

a. Marketing myopia
b. Product naming
c. Marketing
d. Customer acquisition management

5. _____ is a business discipline which is focused on the practical application of marketing techniques and the management of a firm's marketing resources and activities. Marketing managers are often responsible for influencing the level, timing, and composition of customer demand accepted definition of the term. In part, this is because the role of a marketing manager can vary significantly based on a business' size, corporate culture, and industry context.

a. Performance-based advertising
b. Business structure
c. Door-to-door
d. Marketing Management

Chapter 14. Understanding the Model

1. _____ is the realization of an application idea, model, design, specification, standard, algorithm an _____ is a realization of a technical specification or algorithm as a program, software component, or other computer system. Many _____ s may exist for a given specification or standard.
    a. ACNielsen
    b. Implementation
    c. AMAX
    d. ADTECH

2. In economics, business, retail, and accounting, a _____ is the value of money that has been used up to produce something, and hence is not available for use anymore. In economics, a _____ is an alternative that is given up as a result of a decision. In business, the _____ may be one of acquisition, in which case the amount of money expended to acquire it is counted as _____.
    a. Transaction cost
    b. Variable cost
    c. Cost
    d. Fixed costs

3. _____ is defined by the American _____ Association as the activity, set of institutions, and processes for creating, communicating, delivering, and exchanging offerings that have value for customers, clients, partners, and society at large. The term developed from the original meaning which referred literally to going to market, as in shopping, or going to a market to sell goods or services.

    _____ practice tends to be seen as a creative industry, which includes advertising, distribution and selling.

    a. Marketing myopia
    b. Product naming
    c. Customer acquisition management
    d. Marketing

4. In economics, and cost accounting, _____ describes the total economic cost of production and is made up of variable costs, which vary according to the quantity of a good produced and include inputs such as labor and raw materials, plus fixed costs, which are independent of the quantity of a good produced and include inputs (capital) that cannot be varied in the short term, such as buildings and machinery. _____ in economics includes the total opportunity cost of each factor of production in addition to fixed and variable costs.

    The rate at which _____ changes as the amount produced changes is called marginal cost.

Chapter 14. Understanding the Model

a. Hoarding
b. Product proliferation
c. Total Cost
d. Household production function

5. A personal and cultural _____ is a relative ethic _____, an assumption upon which implementation can be extrapolated. A _____ system is a set of consistent _____s and measures that is soo not true. A principle _____ is a foundation upon which other _____s and measures of integrity are based.

a. Package-on-Package
b. Perceptual maps
c. Supreme Court of the United States
d. Value

6. In the field of marketing, a customer _____ consists of the sum total of benefits which a vendor promises that a customer will receive in return for the customer's associated payment (or other value-transfer.)

Put simply, the _____ is what the customer gets for his money.

Accordingly, a customer can evaluate a company's value-proposition on two broad dimensions with multiple subsets:

1. relative performance: what the customer gets from the vendor relative to a competitor's offering;
2. price: which consists of the payment the customer makes to acquire the product or service; plus the access cost

The vendor-company's marketing and sales efforts offer a customer _____; the vendor-company's delivery and customer-service processes then fulfill that value-proposition.

A value-proposition can assist in a firm's marketing strategy, and may guide a business to target a particular market segment.

a. DefCom Australia
b. Value Proposition
c. Marketing performance measurement and management
d. Relationship management

Chapter 15. Adopting the VCCM

1. _____ is the realization of an application idea, model, design, specification, standard, algorithm an _____ is a realization of a technical specification or algorithm as a program, software component, or other computer system. Many _____s may exist for a given specification or standard.

   a. ACNielsen
   b. ADTECH
   c. Implementation
   d. AMAX

2. The _____ is a performance management tool which began as a concept for measuring whether the smaller-scale operational activities of a company are aligned with its larger-scale objectives in terms of vision and strategy.

   By focusing not only on financial outcomes but also on the operational, marketing and developmental inputs to these, the _____ helps provide a more comprehensive view of a business, which in turn helps organizations act in their best long-term interests.

   Organizations were encouraged to measure, in addition to financial outputs, those factors which influenced the financial outputs.

   a. Balanced Scorecard
   b. Goal setting
   c. Time management
   d. Voice of the customer

3. _____ is a business management strategy, originally developed by Motorola, that today enjoys widespread application in many sectors of industry.

   _____ seeks to identify and remove the causes of defects and errors in manufacturing and business processes. It uses a set of quality management methods, including statistical methods, and creates a special infrastructure of people within the organization ('Black Belts' etc.)

   a. 6-3-5 Brainwriting
   b. Power III
   c. Six Sigma
   d. 180SearchAssistant

4. _____ is a technique used in propaganda and advertising. Also known as association, this is a technique of projecting positive or negative qualities (praise or blame) of a person, entity, object, or value (an individual, group, organization, nation, patriotism, etc.) to another in order to make the second more acceptable or to discredit it.

a. Transfer
b. Sexism,
c. Supplier
d. Micro ads

Chapter 16. Building a Value Map

1. A personal and cultural _____ is a relative ethic _____, an assumption upon which implementation can be extrapolated. A _____ system is a set of consistent _____s and measures that is soo not true. A principle _____ is a foundation upon which other _____s and measures of integrity are based.
    a. Value
    b. Package-on-Package
    c. Supreme Court of the United States
    d. Perceptual maps

2. In the field of marketing, a customer _____ consists of the sum total of benefits which a vendor promises that a customer will receive in return for the customer's associated payment (or other value-transfer.)

Put simply, the _____ is what the customer gets for his money.

Accordingly, a customer can evaluate a company's value-proposition on two broad dimensions with multiple subsets:

1. relative performance: what the customer gets from the vendor relative to a competitor's offering;
2. price: which consists of the payment the customer makes to acquire the product or service; plus the access cost

The vendor-company's marketing and sales efforts offer a customer _____; the vendor-company's delivery and customer-service processes then fulfill that value-proposition.

A value-proposition can assist in a firm's marketing strategy, and may guide a business to target a particular market segment.

   a. Marketing performance measurement and management
   b. Relationship management
   c. DefCom Australia
   d. Value Proposition

Chapter 17. Optimizing the Sanctioned Content

1. A _____ researches, selects, develops, and places a company's products.

A _____ considers numerous factors such as target demographic, the products offered by the competition, and how well the product fits in with the company's business model. Generally, a _____ manages one or more tangible products.

   a. Promotional mix
   b. Product Manager
   c. Power III
   d. Pick and pack

2. _____, sometimes referred to as information richness theory, is a framework that can be used to describe a communications medium by describing its ability to reproduce the information sent over it. It was developed by Richard L. Daft and Robert H. Lengel. For example, a phone call will not be able to reproduce visual social cues such as gestures.
   a. 6-3-5 Brainwriting
   b. Power III
   c. 180SearchAssistant
   d. Media richness theory

3. A personal and cultural _____ is a relative ethic _____, an assumption upon which implementation can be extrapolated. A _____ system is a set of consistent _____s and measures that is soo not true. A principle _____ is a foundation upon which other _____s and measures of integrity are based.
   a. Perceptual maps
   b. Package-on-Package
   c. Supreme Court of the United States
   d. Value

4. In the field of marketing, a customer _____ consists of the sum total of benefits which a vendor promises that a customer will receive in return for the customer's associated payment (or other value-transfer.)

Put simply, the _____ is what the customer gets for his money.

Accordingly, a customer can evaluate a company's value-proposition on two broad dimensions with multiple subsets:

   1. relative performance: what the customer gets from the vendor relative to a competitor's offering;
   2. price: which consists of the payment the customer makes to acquire the product or service; plus the access cost

Chapter 17. Optimizing the Sanctioned Content

The vendor-company's marketing and sales efforts offer a customer _____; the vendor-company's delivery and customer-service processes then fulfill that value-proposition.

A value-proposition can assist in a firm's marketing strategy, and may guide a business to target a particular market segment.

a. Value Proposition
b. Marketing performance measurement and management
c. Relationship management
d. DefCom Australia

5. In calculus, a function f defined on a subset of the real numbers with real values is called _____, if for all x and y such that x ≤ y one has f(x) ≤ f(y), so f preserves the order. In layman's terms, the sign of the slope is always positive (the curve tending upwards) or zero (i.e., non-decreasing, or asymptotic, or depicted as a horizontal, flat line) Likewise, a function is called monotonically decreasing (non-increasing) if, whenever x ≤ y, then f(x) ≥ f(y), so it reverses the order.

a. Monotonic
b. 6-3-5 Brainwriting
c. Power III
d. 180SearchAssistant

6. _____ is the corporate management term for the act of partially dismantling or otherwise reorganizing a company for the purpose of making it more profitable. Also known as corporate _____, debt _____ and financial _____.

_____ is often done as part of a bankruptcy or of a strategic takeover by another firm, such as a leveraged buyout by a private equity firm.

a. 180SearchAssistant
b. Restructuring
c. Market value
d. Power III

7. _____ or personalisation is tailoring a consumer product, electronic or written medium to a user based on personal details or characteristics they provide. More recently, it has especially been applied in the context of the World Wide Web.

Web pages are personalized based on the interests of an individual.

Chapter 17. Optimizing the Sanctioned Content

a. Sexism,
b. Personalization
c. Flighting
d. Complex sale

8. _____ is a technique used in propaganda and advertising. Also known as association, this is a technique of projecting positive or negative qualities (praise or blame) of a person, entity, object, or value (an individual, group, organization, nation, patriotism, etc.) to another in order to make the second more acceptable or to discredit it.
a. Sexism,
b. Supplier
c. Micro ads
d. Transfer

9. In economics, business, retail, and accounting, a _____ is the value of money that has been used up to produce something, and hence is not available for use anymore. In economics, a _____ is an alternative that is given up as a result of a decision. In business, the _____ may be one of acquisition, in which case the amount of money expended to acquire it is counted as _____.
a. Variable cost
b. Transaction cost
c. Fixed costs
d. Cost

10. _____ is anything that is intended to save time, energy or frustration. A _____ store at a petrol station, for example, sells items that have nothing to do with gasoline/petrol, but it saves the consumer from having to go to a grocery store. '_____' is a very relative term and its meaning tends to change over time.
a. Marketing buzz
b. Convenience
c. MaxDiff
d. Demographic profile

11. On an intranet or B2E Enterprise Web portals, personalization is often based on user attributes such as department, functional area, or role. The term _____ in this context refers to the ability of users to modify the page layout or specify what content should be displayed.

Chapter 17. Optimizing the Sanctioned Content

There are two categories of personalizations:

1. Rule-based
2. Content-based

Web personalization models include rules-based filtering, based on 'if this, then that' rules processing, and collaborative filtering, which serves relevant material to customers by combining their own personal preferences with the preferences of like-minded others. Collaborative filtering works well for books, music, video, etc.

a. Movin'
b. Cashmere Agency
c. Self branding
d. Customization

12. _____ describes the situation when output from (or information about the result of) an event or phenomenon in the past will influence the same event/phenomenon in the present or future. When an event is part of a chain of cause-and-effect that forms a circuit or loop, then the event is said to 'feed back' into itself.

_____ is also a synonym for:

- _____ Signal; the information about the initial event that is the basis for subsequent modification of the event.
- _____ Loop; the causal path that leads from the initial generation of the _____ signal to the subsequent modification of the event.

_____ is a mechanism, process or signal that is looped back to control a system within itself. Such a loop is called a _____ loop.

a. 180SearchAssistant
b. Feedback
c. 6-3-5 Brainwriting
d. Power III

13. _____ is defined by the American _____ Association as the activity, set of institutions, and processes for creating, communicating, delivering, and exchanging offerings that have value for customers, clients, partners, and society at large. The term developed from the original meaning which referred literally to going to market, as in shopping, or going to a market to sell goods or services.

_____ practice tends to be seen as a creative industry, which includes advertising, distribution and selling.

Chapter 17. Optimizing the Sanctioned Content

a. Marketing myopia
b. Product naming
c. Customer acquisition management
d. Marketing

14. _____ defines a category of software used by marketing organizations to manage their end-to-end process from gathering and analyzing customer data across websites and other channels, to planning, budgeting and managing the creative production process, to executing targeted customer communications to measuring results and effectiveness. _____ is a superset of other marketing software categories such as Web Analytics, Campaign Management, Marketing Resource Management, Marketing Dashboards, Lead Management, Event-driven Marketing, Predictive Modeling and more. The goal of deploying and using _____ is to improve both the efficiency and effectiveness of marketing by increasing revenue generation, decreasing costs and waste, and reducing time to market.
    a. Advertising media selection
    b. ACNielsen
    c. Electronic retailing self-regulation program
    d. Enterprise Marketing Management

15. _____ is a business discipline which is focused on the practical application of marketing techniques and the management of a firm's marketing resources and activities. Marketing managers are often responsible for influencing the level, timing, and composition of customer demand accepted definition of the term. In part, this is because the role of a marketing manager can vary significantly based on a business' size, corporate culture, and industry context.
    a. Door-to-door
    b. Performance-based advertising
    c. Business structure
    d. Marketing Management

ANSWER KEY

Chapter 1
1. b   2. d   3. a   4. d   5. a

Chapter 2
1. b   2. d   3. a

Chapter 3
1. a   2. d   3. a   4. d

Chapter 4
1. d   2. d   3. d   4. d   5. d   6. d   7. d   8. d   9. c

Chapter 5
1. d   2. b   3. d   4. b   5. d   6. b   7. a   8. c   9. a   10. d

Chapter 6
1. b   2. d   3. b   4. a   5. d

Chapter 7
1. d   2. d   3. d   4. d   5. a   6. a   7. b   8. d

Chapter 8
1. d   2. c   3. c   4. a   5. b   6. d   7. d   8. b

Chapter 9
1. b   2. d   3. c   4. b   5. d

Chapter 10
1. d   2. a   3. d   4. d

Chapter 11
1. a

Chapter 12
1. b   2. a   3. d

Chapter 13
1. b   2. d   3. d   4. c   5. d

Chapter 14
1. b   2. c   3. d   4. c   5. d   6. b

Chapter 15
1. c   2. a   3. c   4. a

ANSWER KEY

Chapter 16
    1. a   2. d

Chapter 17
    1. b   2. d   3. d   4. a   5. a   6. b   7. b   8. d   9. d   10. b
    11. d   12. b   13. d   14. d   15. d

www.ingramcontent.com/pod-product-compliance
Lightning Source LLC
Chambersburg PA
CBHW080744250426
43671CB00038B/2870